LIFE AFTER EASTER

*Mystagogia
for
Everyone*

PAMELA SMITH

Paulist Press
New York/Mahwah

Copyright © 1993 by the Sisters of Sts. Cyril and Methodius

All rights reserved. No part of this book may be reproduced or transmitted in any form or by any means, electronic or mechanical, including photocopying, recording or by any information storage and retrieval system without permission in writing from the Publisher.

Library of Congress Cataloging-in-Publication Data

Smith, Pamela, 1947–
    Life after Easter: mystagogia for everyone / Pamela Smith.
       p. cm.
    ISBN 0-8091-3379-2
    1. Eastertide—Meditations. 2. Catholic Church—Prayerbooks and devotions—English. 3. Devotional calendars—Catholic Church. 4. Paschal mystery—Meditations.
    I. Title.
BV55.S55   1993
242'.36—dc20   92-21195
                                                          CIP

Published by Paulist Press
997 Macarthur Boulevard
Mahwah, NJ 07430

Printed and bound in the
United States of America

DEDICATED TO

*the Engleman brothers and Charlie Allabaugh,
for their commitment to lay ministry and their
steady support in prayer*

*and SMP, for her encouragement, hours of listening,
meticulous proofreading, and steadying friendship*

Introduction

As the days lengthen, and the green of leaves and the pastels of blossoms begin to sprout, and birds begin swiping strands and string and old grass and loose fuzz to weave their nests, the dark wonderwork of the Easter Vigil comes.

Amid light and water and blessings over bread and wine and oil, the "newborn" Catholics are welcomed into the family of faith. Many, most, of them have spent long days in preparing for their initiation and have, indeed, undergone election rites and serious scrutiny. Others have made the journey with them, the professed and experienced Catholics who have sponsored them and have joined them to break open the Word, share prayer, and express the stirrings and the findings of faith. Meanwhile, some folks at home have made a happy Lent, giving themselves over more seriously to scripture, coming in for more frequent eucharist, and spending time on the mature considerations of faith and the spiritual life.

For all of these, there is a need for continuing. Newcomers to the church are offered days of "mystagogia," the days from Easter to Pentecost which call them to further unfolding of the Christian mysteries and to reflecting on their experiences of baptism, confirmation, and communion. "Mystagogia" is a help to the further "growing up" of these already very grown-up people who have professed their belief on the night of new water and new fire.

But there are others among us who may be ready for an after-Easter time of reflection, too, others besides the newly initiated, their sponsors, and the holy ones at home. These others are the many who were brought into the church by eager parents and elated godparents, grandparents, uncles and aunts, but who somehow, over the years, loosened or broke ties. Then, somewhere along the way, under some influence and often amid the drama of passiontide and Eastertime, these rejoined. They are the returned and renewed Catholics, people for whom Jesus has become much more personal and real, people for whom the Father has become—it would seem—more friendly, people for whom the Spirit has come to life as they have taken a second look and have found a meaningful and vibrant church. The renewed among us need our mystagogia, waves of it, too.

These reflections, running from Easter to Pentecost, offer a way of coming again at what we have heard and what we have lived. They spring from the daily readings for the weekdays and Sundays of the Easter season, based on the 1970 Lectionary. The ponderings and prayers here are, then, in harmony with the word and the movement of the celebrating eucharistic community, day by day. Christian initiation groups, Bible study gatherings, the newly arrived, the newly come-back, and individuals in their armchairs who simply want to keep renewing beyond Lent may find them helpful. These offerings are for all of us who seek ways to sustain the momentum of falling in love with the Lord and, with the whole church, falling into the arms of grace.

I. Easter Sunday

Acts 10:34, 37-43
1 Corinthians 5:6-8
John 20:1-9

The Service of Light, the long liturgy of the word with its leisurely walk through creation, covenant, call, and Christ, the ceremonies of water and oil, the alleluias, and the late-night eucharist have concluded, and it is sunny day. Those of us who come again to church on Easter morning hear repeated the story that spread "all over Judaea" about that man from Nazareth, Jesus (Acts 10:36-43). We are invited to church to celebrate the story with "the unleavened bread of sincerity and truth" (1 Corinthians 5:8).

Many of us have lived numerous Easters but can fix on only one or two or three that were full Easters, in some way or other a turning point for us. We may remember many chocolate bunnies, colored eggs, new dresses, pastel straw hats (which we liked or didn't like, ad lib), stiff white shirts, strangling ties, stupid suits, and family pictures. "Old" Catholics recall the long communion lines, the unveiling of purple-draped statues, and the unsilencing of glorias, alleluias, organs, and bells. Today, whether we are old Catholics or new, we may notice the paschal candle, the white and gold, and lilies upon lilies. We use rich, varied instruments as we sing with this year's stronger, more mature voices. But there are still probably only two or three special Easters we can call to mind.

One person's Easter may be like this one:

In the early 1970s I lived in Bethlehem, Pennsylvania, and found, in a Puerto Rican parish, a very-much-alive church. One late winter day, as I walked past the now-demolished New Merchants' Hotel (which was a hangout for derelicts, drunks, and lonely old men), something inside me spoke of Jesus: "He is still alive"—in the midst of the unwashed and the not too freshly shaven. I think it was after that experience—which, by the way, did not have one touch of the dramatic about it—that the resurrection became real and personal to me. He is alive. He is still alive. He is alive for me!

A second person's Easter may be more like this one:

I was nearing the conclusion of a thirty-day retreat, so Easter for me happened out of season, but within a cycle of directed meditations. The Jesuit director told me simply to wait for the resurrection to happen—not to "resuscitate" the Lord but to stay by until the tomb opened. All that I can say is that it did, amid summer heat, mowed lawns, untimid rabbits, lumbering skunks and woodchucks, and blue sky puffed with clouds. My chronic back pain was gone and, for the time, I was able to forget that I had diabetes—and that it demanded almost constant attention. There was just life and the good earth and God hovering over all and then simply walking along and enjoying the scenery.

A third person's Easter might come along these lines:

I remember virtually nothing of the afternoon and the evening of that day, though I'm sure I went to church. It was Good Friday. Easter began to arrive that morning for me, as I spent three hours on Folly Beach in Charleston, South Carolina. I strolled, kicking sand, and then sat against heaps of that same sand, walked some more, and then leaned against barrier stones. It was the spring after the hurricane. I sat in the sun, eased, and began floating some heavy inner cargo out onto the wide ocean, the ocean that imaged God so powerfully for me then. As I let the cargo loose on the low waves, I found that I had to let go of any set notions about where the cargo should land or end. For a stretch of weeks after my morning on the long and lonely shore, sprinkled with sand dollars and miniature conch shells bleached white in the post-storm heat, that Easter unfolded for me. My Easter came about as that great ocean of God carried me through resignation from a wearing administrative position, discovery of a new health regimen, the completion of a new book, the takeoff into a new direction in ministry, and the formation of a new friendship.

As we look at today's readings, we can identify with the newly initiated and with the long-time Catholics who have had some awakening, for there is new life in the Lord that comes to us in waves, in walkways, in unexpected inner whisperings. And somehow it grasps us.

We read Paul's admonition, "Throw out the old yeast so that you can be the fresh dough, unleavened as you are" (1 Corinthians 5:7), and we are led to Easter askings:

> What is the yeast in our lives that has gone a long way in raising the "dough" of faith, hope, and love? And where did this dough come from, anyway? Who raised the wheat? Who made the flour? Who prepared and kneaded the dough? And what do we do to say "Thank you"?

As we look at the gospel, and read of the speedy disciples who looked into the empty tomb, "saw and believed," we are faced with more "review" questions:

> Where have we found that we could believe—even though we certainly did not understand? What have we known for no explicable reason?

And when have we somehow trusted a divine intuition? Where have these moments of faith come from? With what ordinary experiences of confidence, trust, insight, and friendship can we compare them? And where else should we be looking?

Thank God, Easter goes on.

Lord of new life and dawn joy, give me glad awakenings. I am grateful for your life-signs and the Easters that have been most preciously mine. Keep raising me, with grace.

∽

2. Monday of the Octave of Easter
Acts 2:14, 22-23 and Matthew 28:8-15

Easter Monday may be a day of changes: snow in the morning, a warming around noon, dark clouds and then rain, a rainbow at mid-afternoon, and a crisp chill at night. With all its variety, perhaps even a parish funeral, it is a good day to look at *quality* of life. Easter not only proclaims life—rich life, full life, everlasting life; it also asks a personal question: What is the quality of *my* life?

Often we really don't know, and the older we get the less ready we are to trust a prompt answer. We are more likely to trust the questions. Several excellent ones for today—suggested by the readings—are questions about time: how we have used time in the past; how we use time right now—and how present we are to the present; how we will use time in the future. In the *Confessions*, St. Augustine wrote about time in the divine, kairotic sense—from the "eternal now" perspective—as the presence of time past, the presence of time present, and the presence of time to come.

Today's readings ask us to look at our quality of life and at our use of time with this triple focus.

Peter quotes Psalm 16 in proclaiming Jesus' resurrection and its impact: "You have taught me the way of life..." (Acts 2:28). The past is present in what we have been shown and what we have long known. So how have we followed the path, and when have we veered off? And, bringing that to the "now," how have we conspired to thwart our own wayward tendencies to detour or fork off again?

The Lord suddenly, from out of nowhere, stands before the thrilled and awestruck women and pronounces "Shalom!" (Matthew 28:9) His presence is peace, in the present tense. So where is our personal peace right here, right now? Where is our collective peace, as church? as human family? Can we feel it, find it, believe it, carry it about? Is peace with us today?

And the Lord gives a command about the resurrection news and its aftermath. The women are told to advise the disciples "that they must leave for Galilee; there they will see me" (Matthew 28:10). We are sometimes quite aware that we both see and don't see. There are times when we have fairly sharp intelligence and times when we have trustworthy, accurate intuitions; there are also times when we are hopelessly myopic, astigmatic, blurred with cataracts. How attuned are we to our promised future? What do we hope to see? What do we expect to see? What, or, better yet, whom do we pray to see?

The path has already been pointed out. The peace is an ever-present pledge and gift. The vision is above the horizon line, over a greening hill—like an April rainbow.

Lord, help me take the path you have long ago shown, and let it lead me to You. Lord, let me walk always in your peace, here and now, present and confident. And, Lord, illuminate me with a vision of all that, with you and in you, can be.

∾

3. Tuesday of the Octave of Easter

Acts 2:36-41 and John 20:11-18

In his *Autobiography* Benjamin Franklin tells of a youthful project he devised whereby he might progress in virtue. He made his virtue list, set goals for himself, focused on the virtues one at a time, and gave himself checkmarks or "gold stars" when he thought he could credit himself with visible results.

Today's reading from Acts doesn't give us a checklist or a chart for spiritual progress, but it does offer a sort of formula. Reform of one's life and baptism in the name of Jesus make up the mixture which will yield the desired results, promises Peter (in Acts 2:38): the forgiveness of sin and the gift of the fullness of the Spirit. Like the millions or billions who have been baptized, we come to know that the reform—the redirecting, the reshaping—of our lives is an ongoing concern. Unfortunately, Peter doesn't tell us quite *how* to accomplish it.

Alongside the empty tomb, Mary, in the gospel, weeps because she can't locate the Lord. Then the gardener speaks her name and she recognizes the Teacher. His directions are blunt:

1. Don't cling.
2. Go tell the others that "I am ascending to my Father and your Father, to my God, and your God" (John 20:18).

She lets go, rushes off and tells, exclaiming first that she has *seen* the Lord.

The commandments are clear enough and so, really, are the invitations presented by the Lord (as in the sermon on the mount). When we ask how to reform, to see, and even to ascend, we don't find a map, a star chart, or a checklist laid out specifically. What we do find is an invitation to prayer. No matter how many times we hear it, no matter how many times we are urged to it, we keep having to relearn, we keep having to be retaught by the Teacher the importance of relating—to his Father and our Father, to his God and ours. It is not so much a matter of numerous prayers or spillings of dire personal stuff as it is a matter of sitting still for a while. We don't get anywhere with sin or with our gifts if we don't rest a bit in the quiet of God's nearness. We need some late nights when there are only stars to watch and some early mornings when the only sounds are distant traffic, trees stirring in cool breeze, and a few birds twittering. We need to walk around a bit, or pause and sit, without saying a thing, if we are to hear any news of God at all. In such moments begins our reforming.

God, draw me into your garden—for stillness, for soundings in you, for certainties that strengthen and reshape me. Let me listen quietly and talk confidently with you, as you teach me.

∽

4. Wednesday of the Octave of Easter
Acts 3:1-10 and Luke 24:13-35

Daily mass becomes a habit with some few people only with age or entrance into a religious community. Before that it may be a Lenten habit only, if it is ever a habit at all. Oh, daily mass attendance may happen in occasional outbursts of fervor—after sacramental occasions, in the aftermath of a gripping retreat, at some time of crisis or exultation. But the habit tends to be short-lived. At some point, however, daily mass can become so important to some of us that life is very empty on the rare day when we cannot be present for liturgy. Despite the predictable drowsiness of some of the dozen or two regulars at an early morning mass, we continue to find something there that is new, vital, and awakening.

Today's readings say some significant things which pertain to liturgy. First of all, there are "two or three gathered." Two apostles, Peter and John, meet a crippled beggar at the "Beautiful Gate" of the Temple. Two disciples, Cleopas and a friend, meet the stranger who walks with them, explicates the scriptures, and breaks bread with them in Emmaus. The Lord IS where the two or three are.

There is healing in both stories: the crippled man's feet and ankles are strengthened, and he walks; the disciples' hearts burn within them, and they finally recognize the risen Lord. Both stories end with the praise of God and rejoicing.

There are commands: "Look at us!" and "Walk!" (Peter to the beggar). There is a chiding: "You foolish men! So slow to believe all that the prophets have said!" (the stranger to the disciples on the road, Luke 24:25). There is begging: for alms, and for the gift of a wise man's presence ("Stay with us!"). The cripple walks, and the disciples are rerouted and fed.

As we look at these two stories of visitation by God, it is enough for us to pray merely for the gift of attentiveness ... to today's liturgy, and then tomorrow's, and then those of *all* of our tomorrows. ...

Lord, give me assurance of your presence as I gather with the two or three. Let me look at you and at the holy ones who have gone before me. Let me walk more strongly along the road where you are. At today's mass, help me to hear and heed your requests of me and your remindings. And let me present to you all my heart's beggings. If I do nothing else, let me take the bread you have blessed and broken and eat it with a still and certain recognition. Let me be more filled with you each moment, each day.

∽

5. Thursday of the Octave of Easter

Acts 3:11-26 and Luke 24:35-48

Peace and perfect health are what all of us would like to have in their entirety but enjoy only in portions or degrees. Faith, Peter says, faith in the name of Jesus, is the source of perfect health—a health which is also freedom. Peace, Jesus suggests, comes from touching him.

Both the story in Acts about the aftermath of the healing of the cripple and the gospel narrative about the risen Lord's invasion of the assembly of disciples connect the possibility of health and peace with a suffering messiah and with human sin.

We often think that we're not doing too badly these days, all things considered. But, in light of the readings, we must see ourselves called to look more deeply—at our Achilles' heel (or heels!), at our persistent tendencies to sin, at our specific potential for blowing grace off and away, and even at our ignorance (which Peter says was much to blame for the crucifixion). It is only, after all, in facing the truth about ourselves—about our gifts and good points but also about our shortcomings and chronic weaknesses and blind spots—that we can get in touch with our own deeply personal need for reform, penance, and remission. And we need to confront a topic that we would generally prefer to avoid: the suffering in our own lives, and how on earth that relates to the suffering, dying, and rising of a messiah.

Lord, where do I most need help and grace? Where do I need to be forgiven? And how can I be freed from my amnesia, that so often causes me to forget that my pain and frustration may actually have Easter light within them? Peace and perfect health? Yes, please, in your name, Jesus, and in the name of "the God of Abraham, Isaac, and Jacob, the God of our ancestors" (Acts 3:13).

∽

6. Friday of the Octave of Easter

Acts 4:1-12 and John 21:1-14

The risen Jesus keeps appearing—even after the ascension. Before that grand leave-taking, he kept appearing to them—in a garden, in their prayer room, on a road, on the beach. He would speak, touch, eat. And afterwards he kept appearing in the reminiscences and the actions—sometimes startling ones—of those who had come to believe.

Bob Engleman, who shares Christ as he drives a truck and repairs furnaces, and teaches Christ as he works with his parish's youth and men's Bible study and local evangelization committee in Milton, Pennsylvania, wishes that more of us would visibly bear the fire. He has spoken recently of a radio preacher who seems to be able to stir up anyone, just by the vibrancy and force of his conviction. Peter and John obviously had the fire and knew it. If we knew the fire we had, Bob suggests, we couldn't help but do everything—go to work, go fishing, eat breakfast, chat, even keep quiet for a bit—"in the name of Jesus Christ the

Nazarene, whom you crucified, and God raised from the dead" (Acts 4:10).

The resurrection has had its lasting, its centuries-drawn-out, effects, but it also had its immediate excitement when it happened. Peter and John were excited and got others excited about the aliveness of the living Lord. The seven disciples who went fishing got excited and expressed their excitement when they recognized the Lord. One cried out, one jumped into the water, the others drew ashore and knew and ate.

For all of us it would be a blessed gift to be able to recognize the risen One in the day-to-day and in the unexpected opportunity. If only we were able to exclaim, "It is the Lord!" with meaning and frequency—not so much in our words as in our whole being.

Lord, what can I do today, deliberately, in your name? And how many times will I see that it is you in the midst of things? I know, after all, that you are "the only one" by whom "we can be saved" (Acts 4:12).

7. Saturday of the Octave of Easter

Acts 4:13-21 and Mark 16:9-15

The Lord has an interesting habit of using people with low credibility ratings. The priests and the elders in Jerusalem were very much aware that Peter and John "were uneducated laymen" (Acts 4:13). Mary Magdalene had a reputation which she had not yet lived down, and she probably seemed given to excesses of sentimentality. The two who had retraced their steps and forgotten about their reason for going to Emmaus just didn't make a great deal of sense when they talked about meeting someone whom they were sure was the deceased Lord, even though he didn't look at all like him. The Eleven themselves got lectured "for their incredulity and obstinacy" (Mark 16:14). They were not a crew likely to be entrusted with a top-priority job.

But all these poor-choice people were the very ones chosen. "Go out to the whole world," he said, "proclaim the gospel to all creation" (Mark 16:15). The Jewish elders were beside themselves and could not figure what to do with them.

We might find ourselves wondering about those whom we, or church people around us, might be disinclined to believe. Some folks criticize the Polish pope. ("He just doesn't understand America or Americans.") Some turn off the gadflies and itches. ("Those women, those minorities, those diocesan employees, those unionized lay teachers, those permanent deacons.... They always have to make an issue.") Some dismiss the pokings and proddings of members of their parishes, their advisory boards, their committees. ("If you ask me, they can't leave well enough alone.") And others write off as irrelevant the cursillistas, the charismatics, the Medjugorje groups, the crowd at NCR, the Search retreatants, the Marriage Encounter couples, the Blue Army, the Legion of Mary, the members of Pax Christi U.S.A., etc., etc., etc. ("A bunch of fanatics!") That's the stuff that goes around.

Meanwhile, people who talk too much and people who barely talk at all, people who pray in tongues at seven-hour prayer meetings and people who look for hermitages in New Mexico or the Catskills, people who hold positions of authority and people who do some hours of prison ministry (like Charlie Allabaugh) after their workday as janitors is over: all of these have been missioned to proclaim the good news.

Who might be the less-than-likely ambassadors of Christ among us today? And whom have we written off because they don't live up to our standards of credibility? And what if one of us is called, qualified and capable or not, to share something of what we have heard and seen of God? Isn't that what we were confirmed for?

Lord, open my eyes to your notion of credibility, and help me to acknowledge that the Spirit works wherever she can and will.

8. The Second Sunday of Easter
Years A, B, and C—John 20:19-31

There are days when peace comes with perfect ease—a day, let's say, when a chilly April has suddenly exploded into a summery weekend: when the spring-thawed water tumbles down the face of cliffs; when families get their small boats once again afloat; when a meeting is shorter than expected, productive, and affable; when one goes for a bright, breezy ride to see—or, better yet, bring home—a friend.

But today's gospel makes it clear, with its thrice-repeated wish, that peace is the Lord's *permanent* will: "Peace be with you," he says.

What we read here is a matter of confession and confidence.

The passage which begins "Receive the Holy Spirit..." is the age-old basis for the Catholic sense of sacramental confession. The older we get, the more some of us come to appreciate it. We find that no matter how Christian we fancy we are, we never lack for something to say to a confessor or spiritual director. There always seem to be knots to untie, tangles to unravel, squiggles to straighten out. Of course, we converse with God about these. But God habitually assures us not only of forgiveness but also of the understanding and the possible new approaches which might be revealed to us through an intermediary. Enfleshing the reality of God's love—speaking his word with a human voice, touching with a tangibly healing hand—seems to be what the church is all about. And, in the midst of confessional challenges, we do find peace.

There is also the question of confidence. It isn't surprising to notice that people seem to feel the farthest from peace when they feel betrayed or befuddled by reality—not sure what to do, whom to believe, where to place trust, what to think, how to go on. Thomas gives a few clues:

Clue #1: Ask for what we need. (We may get it directly, with "proof" as he did, or indirectly.)
Clue #2: Believe—and do so on others' testimony, since they just may be more on target than we think. (The witnesses to the resurrection didn't appear to be authorities on anything, but they were closer to the Truth than Thomas was when he was skeptical of their shared experience.)
Clue #3: Get with a good group. (The time when Thomas was with them, he saw for himself.)
Clue #4: Accept help—gospel help, people help, prayer help. ("These are recorded so that you may believe..." John 20:31).
Clue #5: (The best of all!) *LIVE!* (Don't lose sight of the fact that the Old and New Testaments call us repeatedly to "choose life," to "have life to the full," to "have life in Jesus' name.")

Today, on this Second Sunday of Easter, this may all seem utterly simple, achievable, and clear. Tomorrow or the day after tomorrow, however, we may need a lot to fall back on—the remembrance of *faith* and *forgiveness*—to keep the peace.

Father, forgive me, and keep me honest enough to know that I need not only your grace but human guidance and reassurance. Keep my relationship with your mercy and your compassion horizontal as well as vertical.

9. Monday of the Second Week of Easter
Acts 4:23-31 and John 3:1-8

The wind blows and the Spirit shakes the house, and we don't know why or where it has come from or where or when it will end. We just know that it is. The beat of the spring gusts gives strength to the awakening, budding trees. The breath of the Spirit gives an idea, an urging, and we are prompted to some action. Not that we quite understand it.

Peter and the gathering of believers asked for assurance, healing power, and the gift of signs which would speak to those who did not yet know. Nicodemus, we hope, eventually understood and asked for baptism. What he had, and what the apostles had, was an ability to ask—in questions and in prayer.

We cannot know where the wind might blow or the Spirit might move today as we go about our predictable activities, but we can ask for the grace to go along, sure of God's power and attentive to whatever hints of the Spirit we might hear.

Lord, may I be born again each day in whatever way I need to be born—given new eyes to see, new strength and form to be able to do the small tasks you give me. May I be filled and refilled with your Spirit—like a sail in brisk wind—so that I will know you are carrying me along, giving me more than my own power to go on. Stretch forth your hand. . . .

10. Tuesday of the Second Week of Easter
Acts 4:32-37 and John 3:7-15

"Do not be surprised when I say: You must be born from above," Jesus informs Nicodemus (John 3:7).

Sometimes being around a run-down area of a city for a while gives a dramatic awareness of our collective need for a second birth. We can so easily, it seems, become disconnected and disorderly. We have drunken fights in the middle of the night and smash bottles on the sidewalks. We graffiti walls and mug old women. We make cheap whiskey, snortable coke, or the favorite drug of the week our god. We sit on park benches in despair and watch other people rummage through the trash for supper.

In Philadelphia, near the Museum of Art, however, children wade and splash in the public fountains every summer. They pretend that the fountains are their swimming pools, and they play. The city and the city's police let them. Many of them are obviously deprived kids. But for some morning, afternoon, and evening moments, they are able to enjoy the pleasure of cool, flowing water. It is baptismal, a release from drudgery and want and grime and empty home lives.

In the early church, the real baptism—not just a few child's play dips in the cool Jordan (or Tiber or whatever)—had heavenly effects. The newly christened *felt* "born from above," and it transformed the way they lived each day's taut existence. They were no longer turned in on themselves or trapped in the dark tunnel of personal need. Luke tells us that among them "everything they owned was held in common" (Acts 4:32), the needy were provided for, and the prosperous handed over their property or their proceeds for general use. The Amish today raise each other's barns, and small Christian communities rally around at least with food and drink and company when death or disaster strikes someone. But most of us cannot begin to imagine how to go about a wholesale social reorganization along genuinely baptismal lines. We just see the outcomes of *not* doing it: an escalating crime rate, patterns of addiction, victimization of the weak, violence as a mindset as much in our Congress as in our streets. Where do we begin our new birthing?

Lord, let me live today at least as a reborn person, with my eyes on the needs of others. Give me, if only in one situation, the perspective of heaven. And let me see how I should respond and where I best fit into the grand, cosmopolitan plan of salvation.

∾

II. Wednesday of the Second Week of Easter

Acts 5:17-26 and John 3:16-21

In contrast to the powerful Easter images of lit candles and the dazzle of dawnlight falling on an empty tomb, we confront today the reminders of prison and darkness. Prison, however, simply could not hold the apostles. At night an angel, a being of light, broke open the jail and sent them out to preach again. The burning in their hearts kept turning into words, and their light could not be dimmed.

The Lord cautioned Nicodemus, however, that it is a sadly human thing to prefer darkness—the darkness of unbelief or ignorance or the sin we won't let go of. Undaunted, the Lord keeps inviting us into light—the light of the Son, the light of faith, the light of a life that "does the truth" (John 3:21).

As we consider the choices, darkness or light, prison or

freedom, we should not be too ready to assume that we have already made our choices and that everything else is a foregone conclusion.

Every now and then we have to ask what prison or prisons we still might be locked in. The prison doesn't have to be as obvious as narcotic addiction, or lechery, or outright unbelief. It might be a more subtle matter of stubbornness, or prejudice, or excessive concern about personal popularity, or good old American status-seeking.

With this we also need to ask where we might be in the dark. It need not be in a subterranean windowless dungeon. It might just be a shadow. What is it that we would rather not let be sufficiently lit up that it might be seen? What are we hiding?

> *Lord, open whatever prisons I might be in, and let your light flood whatever corners are still darkened in me. I mean this. Please.*

12. *Thursday of the Second Week of Easter*
Acts 5:27-33 and John 3:31-36

Catholics in this century—in America, at least, if not in the whole west—have acquired a reputation for being very cooperative people. Being a good citizen, a good churchgoer, a good club member, a good worker, a good parent, a good son or daughter, and a good kid in school all seem to come with the territory of being a good Catholic. While we have worked quite hard at being good team members, we have not put much effort into being, or even knowing when to be, good conscientious objectors. We generally seem to pay our taxes and our dues without asking if the money is rightly spent. And we go off to wars, after our President has said some persuasive things on television, without pausing to take a giant step back to get a broader look and without ever asking if this particular war—or any war—is just.

Peter and the apostles at least knew that they were in enemy territory. That knowledge helped them to conclude early on that "obedience to God comes before obedience to [humans]" (Acts 5:30).

As we become more adult in our faith, we find that the questions of what to obey and whom to obey, what to resist and whom to disobey, get more complicated. Yes, surely, Jesus said many things that suggest virtue in submission and compliance, but he also stood forcefully against the forces of hypocrisy, destruction, and evil. And he sharply contrasted the will of God to the "earthly way" (John 3:31). Discerning which is which, here and now, day in and day out, can get very fuzzy. The basic Christian principles—love, truth, humility, compassion, justice, and the whole array—remain in essence the same. But the applications become befuddling. Is it obedience or disobedience to "hang in there" with an institution or a workplace which means well but has some of its values clearly askew? Is it obedience or disobedience to say "Enough!" and disengage a connection with a person or group one has pledged one's life to when the relationship becomes just too much? What is kindness, and what are the demands of tough love? What is integrity, and where is tolerance called for? What can we hope to influence for good, and what threatens to pull us into a damaging way? When and how might noncompliance and intolerance be our morally imperative response?

Good versus evil, ego versus other, good versus better, God versus me or us: which way is which? and what is what?

Discernment is indeed a gift, but, beyond that, it is a Christian necessity. We need it, and we need to know more about it. Why? Because we *do* want to obey God, and we do want the obedience to the Son that promises us "eternal life" (John 3:36). The unsettling possibility is that, if we go on with our unexamined personal and national lives, we may not even realize it when we are making a choice.

> *Lord, you promise that you give to us what you yourself possess, the gift of the Spirit "without reserve." Please give that wise, discerning Spirit to me. Remind me that I need to question, to examine, and to pray as I think things through carefully.*

∼

13. Friday of the Second Week of Easter
Acts 5:34-42 and John 6:1-15

Now and again we meet up with God's power to multiply—barley bread, fish, believers, a movement. Sometimes it can be amazing, stupendous. We're down and out, or sick and lonely, and we find out that we have more friends than we knew we had. Sometimes it can be overwhelming and draining. The number of jobs we're asked to do in a limited period of time, the places we should be simultaneously, the mob of people who want us to lend them something—if only a willing ear—can come at us so rapidly that we want to run off. Jesus may have felt that way when the "large crowd followed him, impressed by the signs he had done in curing the sick" (John 6:2). Both readings today assure us, however, of God's elasticity, God's quite astonishing methods of working in increments.

The cool cucumber in the Sanhedrin may not have realized what a loaded statement he had made when he suggested the laissez-faire approach to the new Christian phenomenon. He figured that they would destroy themselves or flourish, depending on whose spirit was moving them. We know that *the* Spirit was at work, so of course the movement continues two thousand years later and includes a large percentage of the world's billions. The same Spirit fed the hungry five thousand. Maybe it was all marvel and wonder, but maybe—as many scholars and homilists have conjectured—the people really did have all that food with them, cached away in satchels and pockets for themselves. Maybe Jesus' insistence and the little boy's surrender motivated them to put everything they had out for the communal sharing.

That is God's multiplicative character.

We are asked, today and every day, to do what we do "for the sake of the name" (Acts 5:41) and to let people know that our being one of the followers of the messiah matters. We usually don't, and perhaps can't, know the effects, the widening ripples, of whatever we play out, whatever stone we drop into the human pool. Today, and every day too, we are called to break the bread of ourselves, to share the bread, to *be* communion. We don't, and perhaps can't, know if we ever have fed or ever will feed a famished crowd. But we have to give whatever we have that can and should be given. We have to trust that it will be enough . . . and that *none* of us will self-destruct or die of starvation.

Whatever is given into God's hands seems to have an uncanny way of replenishing and reproducing itself. It is like the remarkable regenerative powers of the flatworm: it can regrow severed parts and, if cut into large enough pieces, grow a new flatworm from each part. We heard once in biology class that that was the way with planaria, and we can see, too, that it is the moral of the story of the early Christian community as well as the lesson of the boy with the barley loaves and fish. Today it has to be the moral and the ethic of church and eucharist. Whatever is given away, whatever is given over to God's "enterprise," tends to multiply and multiply. That must be our moral, the ethic of every single one of us.

Lord, help me loosen my grip so that I may drop everything into your open hand. Make me a more lavish, as well as a more cheerful, giver.

∽

14. Saturday of the Second Week of Easter
Acts 6:1-7 and John 6:16-21

Whether we were baptized at the age of three weeks or shortly after our 58th birthday, most of us surely had no idea that baptism would sweep us into all sorts of other things—questions about the division of labor, let's say, or matters of justice, such as whether the Greek widows got as good treatment as the Hebrew ones. The early Christian community realized in its youth that it not only had to pay close attention to "prayer and the service of the word" (Acts 6:4) but also to simple acts of human caring—acts like distributing food to the hungry and waiting on tables at gatherings of the community. The members of the community thus began improvising, creating new roles, new relationships. We are told that "a large group of priests" were among those who embraced the faith (Acts 6:7), but nowhere does it say that they then took up roles comparable to the ones which they had known in Judaism. We are also told that seven men were chosen for a role of leadership and service—called to be deacons, prayed over, ordained as the apostles imposed hands on them.

By that time, perhaps, the apostles were becoming used to being swept into new things. They had been rowing in a stormy lake once and had been met by the Master walking on the water. Then suddenly the boat was swept aground, even though moments before they had been some distance off shore.

It seems that baptism sweeps us somewhere, even if we ourselves never learn to walk on water. It asks us to see all of life in a different way, and it asks us to look for innovative methods of assuring that justice is done and that people are treated equitably. It asks us to balance our work with prayer, and it asks us to be prudent (as the first deacons reportedly were) as well as open to surprise. Baptism also asks us to listen for a voice: "It is I. Don't be afraid" (John 6:20).

> *Lord, wherever I am swept this day—in action or idea, or in prayer—let it be in your direction. And help me not to fear whatever comes my way. Make me open to creative possibilities.*

15. The Third Sunday of Easter

Year A—Luke 24:13-35
Year B—Luke 24:35-48
Year C—John 21:1-19

The gospel for each Third Sunday of Easter in the three-year cycle somehow deals with eating and feeding. When we take the three gospels together, we find apparitions of Jesus, delayed recognition, gradual comprehension, reassurance, and then bread and/or fish.

In the first part of the Emmaus story, Jesus becomes known in the breaking of the bread and in the recollection of the disciples' burning hearts. In the sequel to it, he appears again, pronouncing peace, inviting the apostles to touch him, and eating. On the road to Emmaus and later, in the room where the group had gathered, the Lord opens eyes and hearts as he opens the scriptures. On the beach by the Sea of Tiberias, Jesus advises the fishermen and cooks a breakfast for them. They already know him when he invites them, "Come and have breakfast" (John 21:12), and Peter nods again and again, "Yes, Lord," as he hears words which hark back to Ezekiel's prophecy of the good shepherd and to his own apostolic call: "Feed my lambs ... Look after my sheep ... Follow me." Peter's heart is opened with love and also, we are told, with the capacity for hurt.

What of this eating and feeding? The Lord, even in his resurrection, is human and hungry enough to eat. The fish have long swum in water, and the bread is broken after it is blessed. The suggestion is that *we* have been bathed in water (baptism) and have been given the full-bodied bread (communion) and are now expected to attest, to witness, and to feed.

Perhaps today it will only be a matter of telling of the meal by singing a wholehearted communion hymn and praying aloud with a friend or neighbor. Or perhaps it will be an unexpected call to minister to someone lonely or pained.

We don't know what, after the liturgy, it will be. But, whatever the day brings, we must hope that we will indeed see the real face of anyone we might feed and know the Lord in anyone who asks, "Touch me . . ." (Luke 24:39).

> *Lord, the day won't necessarily find me walking to the next town, sitting in a supper room, or fishing in a lake. But I pray, Lord, to be able to see your living face. Give me whatever I need to reach out, to feed, to touch your human body, your human need.*

16. Monday of the Third Week of Easter
Acts 6:8-15 and John 6:22-29

Stephen angered and repulsed some people, but he also attracted quite a following. We are told that he "began to work miracles and great signs among the people" (Acts 6:8) and that when he was called up for questioning by the Sanhedrin "his face appeared to them like the face of an angel" (Acts 6:15). There was something exceptional and striking about him, an inner glow or radiance that had a magnetic effect. Just a little less than two thousand years later we still know of him and read his story and have a record of his words. There is something about a great "soul force" that draws—powerfully.

It is even more so with Jesus. He alienated the traditionalists, too, but he could hardly find a moment of privacy once people began to hear of him and experience him. He worked signs and spoke mysteriously of bigger things: "eternal life." If they lost track of him, the crowds went looking—even to the opposite shore of the lake. There was an irresistible attraction about him.

What about us? We must trust—adamantly—that we have in our midst people of radiance and attraction. We must further trust that we know enough to seek them out and listen to them. And then we must pray that we, too, give off something of the radiance of the Spirit. The greatest and most confounding sign we can work is to live lovingly, with our commitment to Christ up front.

We may not have anyone trailing after us, and we may never look much like angels, but we can hope that our influence will draw someone closer to "carrying out God's work" and believing "in the one he has sent" (John 6:29).

Father, let me give testimony, even quietly,to the radiance and magnetic power of your Son. No matter what I do today, let it draw others to him in some way.

∽

17. Tuesday of the Third Week of Easter
Acts 7:51-8:1 and John 6:30-35

There is that passage in which the Lord assures us that if we ask for bread God is not a father who would hand us stones.

Stephen, however, had stones flung at him. He was pounded so persistently and so long that it killed him.

The amazing thing about him—and about so many martyrs whose stories are told—is that he could see beyond the violent event, the hatred and the harm and the murder, to another dimension. As the angry assault was about to begin, he declared, "Look! I can see heaven thrown open, and the Son of man standing at the right hand of God" (Acts 7:56). As he died, he commended his spirit to the Lord and asked forgiveness for his assailants.

Stephen was not handed a pleasant dish, but he obviously had received the "heavenly bread" that enables the spirit to survive even while the body dies.

Do I really believe, Lord, that your bread will sustain me through trauma, or even a bitter death? Am I asking often enough to see beyond the appearances of things? Lord, as I again receive you, help me both to be sustained and to see.

∽

18. Wednesday of the Third Week of Easter
Acts 8:1-8 and John 6:35-40

Al was a deathbed conversion case. Dying of cancer, he made peace with his estranged son and with the church he had succeeded in avoiding for the better part of forty-seven years. He had been baptized and confirmed as a child; he had received communion and gone frequently enough—for a while—to confession. But he got tied into business shenanigans and then, rumor had it, into arrangements with the Mafia. He didn't see any point in sacramentalizing his marriage, even though something moved him to send his children to Catholic schools. Some people heard of Al's belated reconciliations and shrugged. Knowing that death is imminent does have a way of reordering priorities. But a few also perceived something miraculous in Al's peaceful end.

Long ago Philip "went to a Samaritan town and proclaimed the Christ to them." He healed cripples and paralytics and even expelled demons. "The people unanimously welcomed the message Philip preached, because they had heard of the miracles he worked and because they saw them for themselves" (Acts 8:5-8).

Someone said something to Al about the Lord, and for some reason he "welcomed the message" and listened. The miracle was not something he saw but something he felt, from inside out. There was some sort of gentling and healing within. It seems that the one or perhaps several he paid attention to were not the hospital chaplain, nor the occasional visitor, and not even the somewhat superstitious wife. The voices that got through to Al were voices in his memory, voices he had once believed—a pious and pleasant old-country grandmother, an affable elderly priest, a smiling and suffering-seasoned uncle, a sister in school, someone on the street, the mother who got him to church in the first place. Childhood faith tends to be direct and sincere. It came back to Al. And with it came Al's awestruck realization that he was in the Lord's memory too: "I will certainly not reject anyone who comes to me" (John 6:37).

There are probably a few inner miracles we all would like to see, a few turnabouts of grace. Can we hope that if someone has, some time back, heard the word and received the bread of life, there is a good chance that the benefit will still be able to bring him or her back?

Holy Spirit of Jesus' memory, bring back the days of grace, the early religious stirrings, the familiar verses and prayers to my mind and to the mind of anyone whose lapsed faith I lament. Make real again the Ultimate Reality we began to touch when we were young, though we may later have ungripped our hands from your own. Meet us with outstretched arms, and welcome your wanderers home.

∽

19. *Thursday of the Third Week of Easter*

Acts 8:26-40 and John 6:44-51

Philip is called to the desert route, and an Ethiopian official is called to water. It begins with the Ethiopian's puzzlement over an Isaiah scroll. Philip becomes his companion, his catechesis, his scripture course, his textbook of exegesis.

What is hard for the Ethiopian to understand was once, we know, almost incomprehensible to Philip, too. But he has learned well and has the magnificent skill of the teacher who has struggled to break through the mysteries of a wonderful subject.

Philip unrolls before the Ethiopian the truth of a sheeplike savior, a slaughtered God, a human risen from the dead. If he could have been sealed in a cave or buried himself in the earth, the Ethiopian, in his enthusiasm, probably would have been. Instead he asks at least to be flooded with water and to begin again.

As the Ethiopian was seized by grace, Philip was suddenly seized for mission—transported from the desert route to Azotus.

Both of them still had to learn in their own lives how they would be led sheep-like and sacrificed, or turned to bread and eaten. It was inevitable, though. The bread of life does get eaten—for one's own "eternal life" but also, and more importantly, "for the life of the world" (John 6:51).

Both would continue to learn. And both would certainly teach—hunger, thirst, immersion, breaking, fulfillment. We may, too.

Lord, quicken and impel me with your Spirit. Let me ask to learn and gladly teach. Let me come to the water and come to eat. Let me be good news.

∽

20. Friday of the Third Week of Easter
Acts 9:1-20 and John 6:52-59

In the reading from Acts, two people have their minds changed, Ananias and Saul. In the reading from the gospel for today, Jesus asks for a new perception, a change of mindset, on the part of a whole group, those gathered at the synagogue in Capernaum. We are not sure how many see in his new way or even comprehend his "bread of life" and "blood to drink" message. We do know that the two men in Acts, however, are shaken violently out of their old way.

With all the dramatics of the episode on the road to Damascus, the temporarily blind Saul comes to see two new things:

1. that Jesus is indeed alive; that the resurrection is not just the pious fantasy of a few imaginative fanatics;
2. that Jesus, in his new risen life, has taken up residence in his followers, in the person of each person;

thus, it is Jesus whom Saul has been persecuting in every single victim.

Ananias has a vision and is commanded out of his reluctance as he hears that what he has "heard from many people" (Acts 9:13) might not be the whole story about a man or his purposes. And perhaps Ananias learns still another perennial Christian truth: that God chooses as his instruments those whom others would consider impossible, unlikely, least qualified. Thus he sees two things too:

1. that reputation and past reports aren't all that reliable in assessing someone;
2. that God can be expected repeatedly to choose and call unexpected persons.

The Lord is the master of new things and surprise, and thus we believe:

- that the dead have not died;
- that the Christ is to be found in present, flawed but faith-filled persons;
- that the Lord wants to change our perceptions, our hearts, our minds (metanoia!);
- that the Lord calls without regard for human notions about prerequisites;
- that he chooses unlikely means to communicate himself (including our communions)!

Lord, today let me receive you in whatever way your aliveness and surprise come at me.

21. Saturday of the Third Week of Easter
Acts 9:31-42 and John 6:60-69

A little north of Dauphin, Pennsylvania, state route 225 intersects with Affection Road. It is shortly before the weeping willows and the farmlands begin, shortly before the fresh-plowed fields in spring that are brown with clumps of mud, several miles before the battered barns begin, one of which wears the worn slogan painted in old red, "Ye must be born again." It is many miles before Berrysburg and Pillow.

All of us want comfortable towns, or at least comfortable homes; nice yards, or at least sheep on the hill somewhere in our lifetime view; good names to come home to—Affection Road, Berrysburg, Pillow. The early Christians were like us in that. While they were enjoying the palpable encouragement of the Holy Spirit, things were good and gentle. But when a kind woman died, a woman outdone by no one in generosity and good will, the beds got mussed, the towns got ramshackle, and the affection didn't know how to withstand mourning. Just this once they got the calm back—as Peter happened along and had another chance to see that the Lord's power was indeed coursing through him. Perhaps it was for them, for the present, till they would have time to learn a bit more about the continuity after death, about resurrection.

Tabitha, like the little girl whom Jesus had raised, got up.

Earlier, when Peter and the apostles had been tempted to turn back in the face of the inscrutable sayings about the "bread of life," the rock of the apostles had wondered aloud, "To whom shall we go?" (John 6:68) He knew that once Jesus had crossed his path there was no Affection Road, Berrysburg, or Pillow that could be home enough for him. Ease could no longer be easy enough.

Lord, what have I had to let go of—what comfort, what security, what simple pleasures—to follow you? And where, Lord, am I with the bigger matters—the separations and disjunctions of death? How do I experience the resurrection or the comeback of someone I've held in affection, even if they never make the dramatic return of a dressmaker (Tabitha) whose name meant "Gazelle"?

22. The Fourth Sunday of Easter

Year A—John 10:1-10
Year B—John 10:11-18
Year C—John 10:27-30

A woman from suburban Connecticut recently remarked that she had a lifelong image of sheep as small, sparkling white, and easy to carry and fondle. Then she came to Pennsylvania farm country and saw the real animals for the first time—scruffy, dingy, clumsy, roly-poly things with twigs and briars and mud caught and matted in their unsheared wool. She couldn't imagine how anyone could handle them.

It may help us to remember what real sheep are like, instead of cartoon, sleepy-time, motel logo sheep, when we come to good shepherd Sunday. The gospels for the day tell us about One who is not only willing to handle a grubby, lumpy, greasy-hooved flock that munches grass down too close to the ground, but who even insists on loving them. In comparing himself to a shepherd, the Lord reminds us that he sees something prized and precious in these domesticated little beasts which hardly happen to please *our* sight up close. We, of course, are comparable to the ungainly and unshorn. We turn out to be lovely in the eyes of the one who watches us at night, and we come to know his voice.

The good shepherd gospels have something to say about larger subjects than sheep and the shepherd who guides them home through a sheepgate. They speak of fullness of life; they present a surprising notion of freedom; and they offer a way of discipleship—a following.

The safe and steady sheepkeeper announces why he has come and what he is dedicated to: the single goal "that they may have life and have it to the full" (John 10:10). By image and implication, Jesus indicates that those who hear his voice and walk his way will find life and fullness. The promise doesn't seem only to be one of eternal life—immortal "grazing" in the pastures of heaven—but also of a fullness of life here and now. That fullness of life becomes possible, no matter what the specifics of our human condition are, because of the assurance that we are lovable and loved by One who is larger than ourselves.

The freedom which the shepherd speaks of is the freedom to give all. He speaks of knowing the sheep, being ready to give his life for them, and accepting other sheep to be led, even those who don't know him or "belong." His arms-wide proclamation is that freedom, in its ultimate form, is a total self-surrender to and for the other.

Following the shepherd is a simple, clear-cut matter for us, if we observe these easy directions:

1. Hear.
2. Know.
3. Follow.

Hear what? The Lord's voice, which is the voice of God within our decibel range.

Know what? That we ourselves are very well-known—by the Father, who knows all and "is greater than anyone" (John 10:29).

Follow whom? The shepherd who speaks, who is one with God.

On good shepherd Sunday, we are reminded, in the end, that it is all one: the life-giver, the lover-God; the sacrificing, selfless Son; and the dingy, awkward, ungainly flock who are beautiful and treasured and even Spirit-filled, among whom we are one.

Shepherd God, carrying me safe against wolves and thieves, thank you for my life and my living—for my washing, my feeding, my place to sleep under your watch and even in your arms. Thank you for finding me worth dying for. And thank you for leading me from here and now to eternity.

∽

23. *Monday of the Fourth Week of Easter*
Acts 11:1-18 and John 10:1-10 or John 10:11-18

"Tanya! Jessica?" These were the questions and exclamations of the Catholic high-school faculty when they heard who some of the people were who had signed up for the vocation retreat at the convent. Apparently they were not the most angelic senior girls.

The Jewish Christians had the same reaction to the Gentiles' response to the good news of Jesus. They wouldn't have expected it. And so Peter had to defend the unseemly practice of going into a Gentile household and eating there. He had to defend it on the divine authority of an apocalyptic dream he had had in Joppa.

The point of the experience, however, was not the dream but the realization that *God,* not some ritual, had "purified" the Gentiles and that *God* had freely lavished the Holy Spirit on them. It was a matter of God's initiative.

And it continues to be God's initiative which calls us to Catholicism, to church ministry, to a lifetime cycle of conversion. It is the Lord who chooses us "other sheep," new ones, possibly unlikely ones. And he lavishes "life . . . to the full" on us. It is an offer we can't resist ourselves, if we are wise. And it is an offer we can't question in others, if we have even a single brain cell of "the mind of Christ."

Tanya! Jessica! You too! And me!

Lord, grant me the memory of your gratuitous gifts to me and a readiness to celebrate your liberal invitations to everyone else. As I count myself among the sheep, I want to notice both how like and how unlike me the others are. I praise your desire for variety!

∽

24. *Tuesday of the Fourth Week of Easter*
Acts 11:19-26 and John 10:22-30

As history tells us, Antioch was the place where the church was first referred to as "catholic," and Acts reveals that it was, even earlier, the place where the disciples, the followers of "the way," were first called Christians.

Everyone, from well-financed televangelists to destitute old ladies in bus stations, can hold forth in some way about what might constitute or characterize a Christian. The gospel indicates, among other things, that being a Christian or being a disciple is somewhat like being a sheep.

The suburban Connecticut woman who was surprised at the yellowishness, the grayness, the dinginess of "white" wool in its walking form added an afterthought. She said that when she finally took in the reality of what real sheep look like she felt a compulsion to scrub them and bleach them until they turned the pristine white she had expected.

Their rough earthiness was such a disappointment that she wanted to do something to "correct" it.

Jesus, however, did not demand on-the-spot pristineness. What he did demand was a knowledge of our need and the recognition of which voice to follow. He demanded our willingness to hear. He seemed quite ready to accept and tend the sheep in their come-as-you-are condition and to whiten the wool *gradually*. The good shepherd gives the impression that he can easily clean up the sheep enough to make them presentable, but that he is not unduly concerned about making them "perfect" in an unnatural sense. He very matter-of-factly trusts that the sheep will come along and that they will "do," no matter how they are. "The sheep that belong to me listen to my voice; I know them and they follow me," he states simply (John 10:27). The point is that they listen to his voice and follow, not that they get it perfectly right or flock in military precision.

The willingness to hear and a readiness to be led was exhibited by some of the Jews whom Stephen met in Phoenicia, Cyprus, and Antioch, and some of the Greeks in Antioch whom the new Christians from Cyprus and Cyrene spoke to. When Barnabas and then Paul came to tend this new flock, they took their time. Acts tells us that they spent an entire year with the church, catechizing, teaching. They took the new converts from where they were and asked of them only open ears and open hearts. Bleached-white immediate purity was apparently no more a requirement for them than it is for us now.

> *Lord, thank you for the long time you have spent and continue to spend. Speak softly, lead me gently, and keep me open always to learn more of your words and your works. Conform me gradually to the sparkling image of you that I may be invited to be.*

25. Wednesday of the Fourth Week of Easter
Acts 12:24-13:5 and John 12:44-50

The very word "mass" tells us that we are a community that is *sent*: we are missionary.

In his most recent mission writings, Pope John Paul II has emphasized that our most compelling mission is to those who have not heard the word at all, to those who live with no local church, no gathering of believers among them or nearby.

But we also hear the cry of the beginning church, the poor church — the bedraggled, shuffling Andeans who gather in a hut of bamboo and straw lashed together with rope and post a clumsily carved sign there, "Iglesia Catolica" (Catholic Church), announcing themselves to the rest of the Peruvian village.

And we know, too, that we are called to personal witness and mission day in and day out to the affluent, the churched, the complacent. We are sent among those who have heard but have not comprehended, to those who have an inkling but no real grasp, to those who wonder but resist.

To whom shall we go? To those who have never heard? To those who have heard in their bare-bones poverty? To those who hear amid much noise and consumerist hype?

It is certainly a matter of personal prayer and vocation, but it is also a concern for the whole discerning church— a church which does today what it did in the days of Barnabas and Paul: engages in the liturgy, fasts, prays, sets people apart and sends them off to *do* the truth, to speak the word spoken first by Jesus, in the name of his missioning Father.

As you have washed me with water, fed me with bread, and cheered me with wine, set me straight, Lord, in my journey. Strengthen me for the day. Let what I do and say, Lord, be in your name and in communion with your people . . . so that all nations are somehow reached and touched.

∽

26. Thursday of the Fourth Week of Easter

Acts 13:13-25 and John 13:16-20

Up above the Pocono Mountain resorts, on the main street of Clarks Summit, Pennsylvania, not far from the winter ski slopes and summer lakes, is the Gee Whiz Fun Apparel Shop. Everything about it proclaims color and excitement and leisure and money. It's not the sort of place that the John the Baptist type would buy into. There's no room in the store for a gloomy, humdrum voice suggesting that repentance might be called for or that someone more important than ourselves might be on the scene and coming along. And, while the clerks are cordial and suave and service-minded enough to suit the customers, it's not a spot where feet-washing would go over well. "No shirt, no shoes, no service," signs on the doors of such stores warn.

Businesses defer to consumers, to our pleasures and tastes. Shop clerks defer to customers, to our whims and extravagances and egos. They do it for their own benefit: for dazzle and profit. John the cousin deferred to Jesus. Jesus deferred to his disciples. John's deference was to the person of the messiah, the person of God. Jesus' deference was to the person of the simple person, to his or her divine and altogether earthly possibility.

Both were sure and integrated and sufficiently in touch

with God that they could declare "I am" without having to dress it up. They could bend before someone else for no motives whatsoever but reverence and care.

They were living out of much more than the moment's gee whiz. What of us?

Lord, make me sure and secure in my service and values. Let your Spirit teach me all the things that matter. Lead me to spend myself well instead of frivolously squandering money. More than anything, let me please you.

∼

27. *Friday of the Fourth Week of Easter*

Acts 13:26-33 and John 14:1-6

It is probably a common enough Christian game to fantasize periodically about what heaven might be like. Not surprisingly, a good many people come up with images of an island paradise: a beach in Hawaii or the South Seas. Skies are always sunny and blue, the clouds are always cottony and soft, the sea is always shimmering and calm, and, while it's hot enough, there is a breeze that fans the sunbather and swimmer all day long. The food is cooked on a driftwood fire, the drinks are long and cool, and all that there is to do is to sit there, stroll there, pick up a shell or two, and design elaborate, benign sand castles.

What it's all about is tranquility and basking.

And the images may really not be all that far off.

The most Godly or holy moments we've had here usually have those two ingredients: tranquility and basking. There's a calm and confidence that descends, a quieting and slowing, a sense that all *will* be well and that there is nothing to hurry about or fear. And there's a sensation of being warmed, gently tanned, covered and held in love—the love of the Father, the sunlight of the Son, the fanning breeze of the Spirit. It is good to be, and all that there is to be is basking.

Those who would prefer an Alpine village, a lifetime glide on skis, and an ideal pack and texture to their snow don't have to worry, though. The Lord says that "there are many places to live in" (John 14:2) in that heavenly realm, and that specifically includes "a place for you"—and, of course, for us and me too!

Paul preached the resurrection, Christ's and ours, in Antioch. It seems that there might only be a catch or two to this dream of heaven that we carry about. One is a caution *not* to; one is an invitation *to*:

1. It is important, Paul warns, *not* to follow the path of "the people of Jerusalem and their rulers" who "did not realize" the Christ and what he meant (Acts 13:27).
2. It is easy, the Lord reminds Thomas, *to* get where he is: by following *his* lead. "I am the Way; I am Truth and Life. No one can come to the Father except through me," the Lord adjures us (John 14:6).

The Father is the ocean we want to swim in, the beach on whose drifts and dunes we want to rest. Or the Father is the slope we wish to ski, with wind and speed setting us a-tingle, the soft snow into which we could easily, harmlessly fall. We are meant to rest, to bask secure in Love . . . and to rise.

Meanwhile, Lord, I wonder—where and with whom do I still fail to recognize you? What signposts along the way, what aspects of the truth, what dimensions of life might I still be missing? Open my mind, my heart, my eyes.

∽

28. Saturday of the Fourth Week of Easter
Acts 13:44-52 and John 14:7-14

Moving on, for whatever reason, is a crisis. We have to change and will change, like it or not, and the work will be hard. Packing, unpacking, realigning our lives, establishing new relationships, adjusting to a new environment and creating some space of our own, blending the familiar (that we have brought with us) with the new (that we find) are just some of the challenges. Once we *have* moved, life is never, and will never be, the same. There are new faces, new sunrises, new jobs, new roadways.

When Paul and Barnabas moved on to Iconium, it was because of jealousy, angry argumentation, and finally expulsion. It was a disaster move, a forced going on. There is nothing too happy about leaving a place because you don't fit, can't work there, have been backed into a corner by a group's determined unwelcome. When Paul and Barnabas moved, it was a necessity. The choice they *did* have was *how* to move. They chose to shake "the dust from their feet" (Acts 13:51)—to leave rancor and disappointment and frustration behind them. They chose to go with good will in their hearts and with eyes alert to new opportunity. Thus they arrived in Iconium free of crippling bitterness and ready to meet new persons and new situations with expectancy and open arms.

Jesus, before he moved on altogether, had something to say about the work to be done in his name. He assured Philip, and the others who had asked, that the Father, through the Son, would empower them to "perform the same works as I do myself, and . . . even greater works" (John 14:12). Greater works . . .

In looking back on what had happened at Antioch and at Iconium much later, the church would know that Paul and Barnabas, despite the pressure of persecution and rejection, had done great work in Antioch. They had brought a gift of faith to the Gentiles there, and the gift had been opened and received with a joy like that of a child opening a Christmas surprise. We are told that in the end, even after they had left, "all who were destined for eternal life became believers" (Acts 13:48), and, through the new believers, the word spread.

At Iconium they were welcomed with joy by a Spirit-filled group of disciples ready to receive more. That, at least, was how it began. Wherever they moved, there was only one way to go: in the way of the Lord.

Lord, guide me in my moves, those happy with opportunity and those clouded with pressure or pain. Help me to remember that any move I make must be in your direction, in your way. Give me confidence that your Spirit, whom I have received, stays behind and also goes with me. Let me trust your Spirit, Lord, to make good on what may look like disaster and to embrace what awaits me in any new place.

29. The Fifth Sunday of Easter

Year A—John 14:1-12
Year B—John 15:1-8
Year C—John 13:31-33a, 34-35

When the question "What do you want to be when you grow up?" is asked of kindergarteners and first graders, some few of them can be counted on to reply that they want to be football players, cheerleaders, and rock stars. Then there are the nurses and doctors, and sometimes one finds a precocious child, like one in a school in Endicott, New York, who not only declares his intention to be a paleontologist but also proceeds to explain what one is and does!

All of us at some time have probably imagined ourselves doing something astonishing, famous, and good. Whether we pictured ourselves conducting *Messiah,* discovering a cure for cancer, or becoming the most altruistic and beloved president of the United States, at some point we envisioned ourselves engaged in splendid endeavors on behalf of the arts, health, progress, and humanity.

In the gospels for this Sunday, the Lord proposes to us that we should and we *can* indeed do great, abundant works of love. It isn't a matter of fantasy but instead of faith.

We can and will do noble works, the Lord promises. We can and will produce abundantly. We can and will manifest to the world the possibilities of love. How?

By living a life "in me" (John 15:4), declares Jesus the Vine, knowing full well that we will branch off individually and differently.

Whether or not our achievements look grandiose or our love appears as extravagant as Leo Buscaglia's or Mother Teresa's, we are called to the greatness that is the *"in"* life of the Lord: *in* prayer, *in* attentiveness to the word, *in* response to persons and present opportunities, *in* touch with lasting spiritual values.

We can live that "in" life in the cab of a truck, across the aisles at the supermarket, or on the way to Katmandu, as long as we live *with* the Lord, *in* love.

Well, Lord, how great a lover am I? Am I doing the most important thing you've given me to do—loving abundantly?

30. *Monday of the Fifth Week of Easter*
Acts 14:5-18 and John 14:21-26

There is a great circle of love, and within the circle is a triangle. The energy of love darts back and forth, one way, then the other, both ways simultaneously along the equilateral sides, and an energy, a heat, a power is given off which sets the circle pulsing as love makes a great and ceaseless circle of its whole diameter and again pulses and gives off power. Concentric circles of pure light radiate out.

That is one way to picture what Jesus says of himself, his word, his Father, his love, his Spirit, and the way he will be revealed to the world. When Judas (not Iscariot) asks the question about why they, and not the rest of the world, have been privileged to know the Lord and his love, Jesus does not directly answer the question. Instead he repeats what he has just said: The measure of your love is your living of all that I have said; and anyone who loves me and acts on that love will be tenderly loved by my Father. And then he tells of the more and more—the understanding, the memory, the light—that will come in the Spirit. Without ever exactly saying it, he tells the disciples that the world *will* come to know him and his love, but that it will not be his direct doing; instead it will be through the Spirit who will fire them.

The darting, pulsing energy of love draws today as surely as it drew a crippled man at Lystra, a priest of Zeus, and a crowd-about-town to Paul and Barnabas. As the healing power of love and the rich word of love drew a following to the two early missioners, they kept insisting that all look beyond, to the Source.

Similarly, when people are drawn to us by our attention, our convictions, our gentleness, our integrity, or our love, we must be careful to direct their gaze and admiration beyond: to the Lord, to the cosmic strength of love, to the Father who loves us, to the darting, circling, pulsing Spirit of Christ's caring even today. For that is where whatever fire and force we have has begun, and that is where we have been fed.

> *Give me, Lord, the good sense always to direct people's gaze past me. It is true that I want to be admired, respected, and loved, but I want <u>more</u> to reveal the love that is beyond me and is everlasting. Feed whatever fire I have, and make me light so that I may sweep the skies for others who are watching and waiting for you.*

∽

31. *Tuesday of the Fifth Week of Easter*
Acts 14:19-28 and John 14:27-31

There is a kind of submissiveness in Jesus—a submission to his people, whom he is concerned about as he wishes them peace and explains the necessity of his departure; a submission, too, to the Father, whom he describes always as "greater than I" (John 14:28). For Jesus the center of attention and the object of respect is always the other.

Paul and Barnabas exhibit a submissiveness to the word, a submissiveness to the impulse of the Spirit. Even after Paul is stoned by some former co-religionists and brought back to himself (as his "disciples came crowding around him," prayerful and protective—Acts 14:20), he goes on to preach even more strongly. Barnabas knows that not only his popularity and prestige but also his life and well-being are at risk, but he goes on anyway, back to Lystra, Iconium, and Antioch, and on to Pisidia, Pamphylia, Perga, Attalia, and then back to Antioch again, where, with Paul, he celebrates "all that God had done with them, and how he had opened the door of faith to the Gentiles" (Acts 14:27).

There is nothing hangdog or wishy-washy about Jesus or about his ambassadors. There is a tremendous assurance, self-sufficiency, and strength. But there is also a submissiveness that comes from faith, a self-surrender to a greater Power and a greater plan.

Today's readings raise questions like these:

- How other-oriented are we/am I really?
- How willing are we/am I to change or modify plans for the sake of a greater good?
- How do we/do I receive a sense of God's direction for each day?
- How, to what, and to whom are we/am I ready to listen?

Lord, Lamb of God, help me to submit to your own greatness and to the greatness of your plan. Give me not only peace but also definite direction.

32. Wednesday of the Fifth Week of Easter

Acts 15:1-6 and John 15:1-8

There are an amazing number of cultural Catholics in America—people born into the faith, raised in families that celebrated first communions and confirmations and weddings with parties and presents, programmed to observe Christmas and possibly Easter, but altogether vague about faith, prayer, and the impact of God on daily, nitty-gritty matters. Religion amounts to a name one automatically fills in the blank space for "religious preference" or what one adverts to when upbringing is mentioned. The cultural Catholic probably has a rosary or two, possibly a statue, maybe a Last Supper, and certainly a crucifix in the house. But one can never be too sure whether the Christ is there somewhere in his or her heart.

Jesus warned the cultural believers of his time that the fate of the barren branch on the tree of religiosity was the trash bag. After a while it is inevitable that what is only thinly, loosely connected falls off. The fruitful branch, however, has been tended and pruned clean—so that it can be even more magnificently fruitful.

The truth of Jesus' saying was manifest in the early church. The barren branches, the culturally religious, some of whom were Pharisees, threatened to stunt growth. They wanted a comfortable faith, and they wanted comfortable companions—believers like themselves in origin, in religious practice, in attitude, in narrowness of vision. Meanwhile the Word himself was pruning, fertilizing, grafting new fruitful branches on the tree. The open and the sincere saw where growth was and rejoiced with the Gentiles.

This poses a stickler for us. Our answers may be difficult, fraught with doubt, discomfort, even fear. But we need to ask: Where and who are the deadwood today? And then: Where and with whom is the new and promising growth happening? Knowing where death is and where life is springing forth will determine which voices we listen to most attentively and where we spend our energies. And it is not just a matter of looking at them (whoever they are) out there. It is also an urgent matter of locating the Pharisee within and stifling him or her. It is a matter of discovering the Gentile whose faith is eager, new, and ever-renewed and then clapping hands and raising alleluias with her, with him.

Jesus, master, be my life-vine. Prune my branch clean and make me fruitful. Let me live in the present and the possible more, rather than in the passing and the superficial. Give me a religion that is deep as my heartbeat and my breath and so much more than just custom or novelty and show. Make me, with your church, grow.

∽

33. *Thursday of the Fifth Week of Easter*
Acts 15:7-21 and John 15:9-11

In the midst of anguish and just before the greatest pain—the abysmally lonely and physically wrenching crucifixion, Jesus talks about living in love and having complete joy. The juxtaposition of love and joy with suffering and grief continues to be one of the greatest Christian mysteries.

Love and joy seem to be habits of the mind and heart. When they are already there, grounded in prayer and in the practice of nonjudgmental human give-and-take, they persist. The love and joy last, even in times of trauma or trial. They also provide a kind of elasticity for our human dealings. Peter and James, with the apostles and elders, resolved a conflict in the early church with this kind of elasticity. They realized that people were not to be pushed, and that Christianity was demanding enough in itself without forcing other prerequisites (like circumcision and keeping kosher). There is something of love and joy when James, after hearing the arguments, begins, "My verdict is, then, that instead of making things more difficult for Gentiles who turn to God, we should send them a letter telling them merely . . ." and so on (Acts 15:19-20).

What is almost inscrutable is that time and time again we Christians tend to cause one another difficulty upon difficulty. Certainly there are criteria for religious education and sacramental preparation, and understandably there are expectations about attendance and participation with community as well as about the general conduct and witness of our lives. But we often have exalted and unrealistic notions about what every other believer *should* be doing. What we find in the holiest people, however, is more a live-and-let-live attitude. It is a mindset and a heartwarmth born of compassion. It is a spirit of welcome for the occasional churchgoer, the disheveled youth, the adult whose life looks a bit "loose," the rumpled man in the last pew, the addled old lady who clicks her rosary beads at everyone, the chronic latecomer, the member who can't be counted on to recall what he or she is responsible for. The saints are remarkable in their love and joy, a very *tolerant* love and joy. Maybe the question of the day is why we are not so remarkable, even though we have been given remarkable gifts.

Lord, loosen and ease the muscles of my heart so that I may receive and keep your love. Massage my being with joy so that I may reach out and touch your others gently.

34. Friday of the Fifth Week of Easter
Acts 15:22-31 and John 15:12-17

When all the elaborations have been taken down like fading holiday garland, and all the doodads have been uncurlicued, one can get down to the essentials in Christian morality. The essence seems to be this: we are called to embrace the other and to reject brutality. Embracing the other means ever expanding our breadth, our capacity for compassion (which goes far beyond tolerance). Embracing the other means taking the person on his or her terms and looking through to the divine potential, seeing, even, with divine eyes. Rejecting brutality means shunning not only the obvious violent crimes but also becoming more and more sensitized to what belittles, demeans, burdens.

Jesus called his disciples to friendship, to a community of love. He announced them chosen for mission, for fruitfulness, for embracing a universe. The expanding church early on realized that it must renounce the brutality of pagan Rome and the subtler brutalities of the Pharisees. Guided by the Spirit, they came to see, too, that they were called to reject any stringency among their members which would lay unnecessary burdens and make unreasonable demands on the new ones in their midst. No, the Gentile converts did not have to observe a special dietary regimen, nor did the men have to go through a ceremonial circumcision. They did not have to obey any law but the essential one great commandment which we have come to call two. Aside from that, they were asked to exercise prudence, common sense, and care in their public conduct and in their private handling of food and sex. There was so much more to focus on, to go for.

"What are we here for?" asked the star-gazers and horizon-watchers through the centuries. "Why have I been chosen and for what?" ask the disciples as they look, one by one, at their habits and hangups, their lives and their loves, their perplexities and their possibilities.

We are here to embrace the other and to learn how better we can do that. We learn our loving slowly . . . slowly. We are here to reject brutality . . . and to know how much patience and reverence it takes to invite persons into the open, into trust.

That, it seems, is the essence of Godliness.

"Love one another as I have loved you" (John 15:12). The Holy Spirit has already decided, and the Holy Spirit knows how. It is left to us to ask and to keep asking and to practice by loving undemandingly, liberally, tenderly— the other, the stranger, the new.

O Holy Spirit, open wide my soul to welcome your friends and to ease their way, wherever their way is, lovingly.

∾

35. *Saturday of the Fifth Week of Easter*
Acts 16:1-10 and John 15:18-21

It is Saturday night in the convent. The house meeting is over, and with it the formal farewells to those missioned elsewhere next year. Bathwater is running, and in the laundry a clothes dryer hums away. One sister has Christian radio on, another is watching sitcoms, and a third is immersed in the latest Chaim Potok novel. They all have their opinions about each other, spoken and unspoken. Everywhere religious people have the same problem, the "sins of the just," which are things like criticism, judgmentalism, trivial—yet not altogether harmless—gossip.

Because of this problem, many of us "religious" people become careful and conformist. We avoid "making waves" unless something really comes down to a matter of conscience. We please and cajole and go along.

It must have been that way among Christians as early as the days of Timothy. He had to be circumcised for the sake of in-house public opinion. "Everyone knew" (Acts 16:3) he had a Greek father but a Jewish mother, so apparently they all thought he should be a Jewish Christian, even though it meant a very belated (and probably embarrassing and painful) circumcision. Paul went along.

Meanwhile, the work of the church, the work of the Spirit, got done. Paul and Timothy communicated the good news to and about Gentile Christians. A vision invited them to Macedonia. The good news moved on and on.

But about this circumcision: the Lord had promised persecution and hatred for his followers. He also promised that the whole—the reign of God and also the church—would be more than the sum of its parts. The church would always be, will always be, greater than the members among us who conform, keep the sisters and brothers calm, go along, and do what is expected. That sort of membership may not be wrong. It does, after all, keep peace and at least keep attention and energy focused on bigger and more consequential things. That seems to be how it was with Paul and Timothy. They made a compromise to public sentiment, which allowed them to save their own credibility for disputes about and discussions of weightier things.

We find ourselves having to make those same judgments today: weighing when we need to attend to our image and acceptability to assure that we will have clout when it will count.

Lord, help me to know when to compromise and conform, even when to please, so that my energy may be poured into larger things. Yet help me, too, not just to be a pleaser. Let me stand for good sense, fair play, and personal integrity. Give me both prudence and boldness in right measure.

36. The Sixth Sunday of Easter

Year A—John 14:15-21
Year B—John 15:9-17
Year C—John 14:23-29

Three scenes from the film *Fried Green Tomatoes* capture unique—and stark—moments of desolation. Not long after the film begins, the young and handsome Buddy Truebloode is mangled in a freakish train accident while his younger sister and his newfound "girlfriend" watch, helpless and panic-stricken. Much later, his little sister, now an adult and the best friend of Ruth, Buddy's childhood sweetheart, stays by while Ruth dies slowly and pitiably from stomach cancer. When Ruth finally does die, the young Ms. Truebloode collapses in an agony of loss on Ruth's still-warm chest, as if to listen for a heartbeat. Finally, very late in the film, a very old Ms. Truebloode signs herself out of a nursing home and heads back to her old property and the site of her "Whistle Stop Café," only to find that her homestead has been torn down without her knowledge or permission. She sits on her suitcase staring at the vacant property. All that she has been able to muster the strength to do has been to put fresh flowers on Ruth's now aged grave.

While *Fried Green Tomatoes* ends with hope (represented by the middle-aged woman who has befriended Ms. Truebloode and wants to welcome her into her own home), these three scenes express poignantly the pain of abandonment. They capture something of the worst of human fears: that we will be left alone by someone we have come to count on; that something we own and hold dear will somehow disappear.

In the gospels read on this Sixth Sunday of Easter, Jesus addresses these fears and pledges himself never to abandon us. He promises a lasting parental love: "I shall not leave you orphans; I shall come to you" (John 14:18). He tells us that he regards us not as subservients, not as slaves, but as "friends," and he swears that we are, in his estimation, worth dying for: "No one can have greater love than to lay down his life for his friends" (John 15:13). He calls peace his farewell and his "gift" and reminds us of an old promise that he will keep: "I am going away and shall return" (John 14:28). He will not, cannot, ever really disappear.

With the Lord there is no tragic ending: no lowering of a dazzling boy's coffin that ends with sad shovelsful of dirt thumping on its lid, no stunned realization that the heart of our best friendship has gone still, no dazed stare at an empty lot and an empty horizon. There is instead an everlasting someone with us, the Lord says, in the person of the Comforter, the Paraclete: the Lord's own reachable, present, and steadfast Spirit.

There is, it seems, only one condition to knowing the Spirit's presence and holding on to it: obeying the Lord's commands, keeping faith with, and being true to his word.

That does not seem much to ask from us. But it is everything.

Lord, let me be so magnetized by the power of your love for me that I will do, day after day, all that you ask me. Let me hold you in your bread and wine, in your holy word, in those you call me to love, and let me know that I am never abandoned, never left desolate, as life presses upon me.

37. Monday of the Sixth Week of Easter

Acts 16:11-15 and John 15:26-16:4

"Come and stay with us," be my house-guests, insisted Lydia, the purple-cloth merchant (Acts 16:15). She wanted the bearers of good news, the ministers of the word, right there with her. She opened her house, as she had opened her heart, to those who bore the bearing of the Lord. She saw through to the house of God within them.

What the story does not say is what would have happened if she had extended an invitation, opened her house, prevailed upon them, even made it clear that she needed them there for awhile, and had been left in silence, with the door ajar and the house empty. It implies that the ambassadors of God, the newfound friends in the Lord, would not do things this way. An enemy perhaps would. A person who has "never known either the Father or me," the Lord had said (John 16:3), might be expected to do anything: bar the way, close a door, even kill. But what he doesn't say is what might happen if people know the Father and the Lord differently. Do they stay in their separate houses and hesitate to step over another's threshold? Do they not even say anything about it?

Among Christians we have separate churches. Among friends we have times when a relationship that was, or seemed to be, goes from dwindling communication to virtual silence. The only one who will keep talking perhaps is "the Spirit of truth" (John 15:26).

What continues to be hard to determine is what the Spirit of truth is saying.... To close the door but let it be known that it's unlocked, just in case someone decides to come and stay a while sometime later?

Lord, let me keep an unlocked door—for friend and neighbor, for stranger and estranged. And let me know when to let be and to wait.

∽

38. Tuesday of the Sixth Week of Easter
Acts 16:22-34 and John 16:5-11

When the jailer receives the surprising gift of faith, the first thing he does is to bathe the wounds of the beaten and chained Paul and Silas. After the baptism (poured not only on the jailer but "all his household"), everyone ate and celebrated exultantly.

What was there to celebrate? Among other things, what Jesus had promised at the Last Supper: a confounding of sin, of the world's notions of justice, and of condemnation. A tough jailer had dropped to his knees, good men had been sprung free from their chains, and nobody pointed a finger or hurled accusations at anyone. A jailer had been shocked into belief and brought everyone at home along with him. As their wounds were being washed, Paul and Silas did not ask the jailer why he had not thought of feeding and tending to their needs earlier.

One of the wonders of Christianity is that newfound faith, or refound faith, often can equip us with the ability to celebrate life in the present tense. Anyone who has done it knows how freeing and magnificent it is to embrace someone—family member, old friend—with whom relations have been strained and simply to rejoice in the newness and potential of today. There is little need to rehash the past, except perhaps where talking will help mutual understanding, prevent the repetition of mistakes, and firm up a new beginning. But there is no need for blame when people are impelled by faith to reconciliation. The wounds are healed in the very moment of embracing.

Paul and Silas most certainly embraced their jailer. Miracles of grace and prayer and faith can move us into one another's arms, even after a long estrangement. It is a gift of the risen Jesus. And it is more than enough to celebrate.

Lord, let me have arms open wide to the present and to the present's persons. Heal me of the tendency to live in the past and to dwell on old hurts. Help me instead to celebrate today's infinite possibilities.

39. Wednesday of the Sixth Week of Easter
Acts 17:15, 22-18:1 and John 16:12-15

College students have their energetic and impatient questions; men and women at midlife have their jaded doubts and reconsiderations; idealists have their disappointments and deflations; everyone sometimes ponders the words of songs: "What's It All About, Alfie?" and is God really watching us, as Bette Midler's poignantly convicted voice sings, "From a Distance"?

In Athens Paul picked up on the desire for God and the multi-directed search resulting from that desire. He observed the altar dedicated to an Unknown God. He noted the universal tendency to "seek the deity" and to hope that "by feeling their way towards him" people might "succeed in finding him" (Acts 17:27), and thus find Life. Before Pilate put the question, Jesus went about answering it one way and then another: "What is truth?" He promised to send a Spirit who would lead and guide us to "the complete truth" (John 16:13)—gradually, as we could stand it.

Nearly two thousand years later, we still wonder and we still seek. Like Dionysius and Damaris, some of us are drawn to a special context for our search for truth, for sense, for direction, for answers: the church. Even while we observe its ragged edges, imperfections, and incompletions, we sense that there is lasting wisdom in the church and a beating heart. It is a place where we can ask and live.

Whatever accretions of time and culture and human limits are there, the church remains, for us who have long been members, and becomes, for those of us who have more recently joined, a place to discover much of what it's all about and to approach more closely the God who can at times seem so distant. Why? Because there is an energy in the church, a "life and breath," as Paul suggests (Acts 17: 25). The God whom we *can* come to meet and to know little by little is not an abstraction or intellectual construct or motionless stone. The God to whom the church walks (on many paths) and whom the church expresses (in so many and such diverse words and works) has qualities that are most familiar to us: movement, pulsebeat, the inhalation and exhalation of air we breathe. "It is in [God] that we live, and move, and exist" (Acts 17:28), averred an intuitive Greek and an admiring Paul.

Whether we are youths looking wide-eyed or an older crowd squinting, we can come to the church confident that we will find Livingness—and a way in. From wanting to know *about,* we can come—eventually or soon—to touch, to *know.* There are enough whose whole lives attest to that.

God, let me come to you not just to settle questions but to live. *As I reach out to touch you, fill me with deep breaths.*

40. The Ascension

Year A—Matthew 28:16-20
Year B—Mark 16:15-20
Year C—Luke 24:46-53

The mission to the Eleven is straightforward: Go to "all nations," "the whole world," even "to all creation" to tell the story, to preach and teach.

The event of the ascension itself is paradoxical, however. Was the moment so enrapturing, so consuming, that later they couldn't remember quite where or how it had happened? Was it in Galilee or Jerusalem? Or was it outside the walls of the holy city a bit, at Bethany? And what does one make of the simultaneous absence and presence, disappearance and indwelling, of Jesus? While he passes from their sight, he promises to remain "always; yes, to the end of time," Matthew tells us (28:20). Mark attests that the Eleven indeed had a felt sense of the truth of his continued presence. As they went about—everywhere—they could feel and almost touch "the Lord working with them and confirming the word by the signs that accompanied it" (Mark 16:20). And Luke recounts that even as the precious Master passed from view, the disciples "worshipped him," dropping down in prostration, in an awed gesture of reverence, and then "went back to Jerusalem full of joy" (Luke 24:52)—an uncanny joy.

The moment is a holy commencement exercise—an end and a beginning. It is a lover's experience of the ability to depart and to stay simultaneously. His absent staying is more than a fond note which one finds in the suitcase while out on the road (though the scriptures can and do make for wonderful love letters!). And it is more than vivid memory played back in daydreaming or retelling. No, it is a *real* presence, invisible yet communicated in tangible symbol; unique, indescribable, yet in many ways the same for each who detects it. The presence, the staying, is the baptismal and confirming experience of being Spirit-filled, and the lastingness of being Spirit-filled manifests itself recurrently—in great ways and small, in whole ecclesiastical events and personal ones. The real staying is eucharist—not only the eucharist of bread and wine blessed and divided at every moment around the globe (and how often do we remember that mass *is* always going on somewhere?) but also the eucharist of the human person, the face and the eyes we meet. That paradoxical presence of the Lord is an event of our intuitions, our calmings, our holy impulsions, our prayer.

But it doesn't end in a reminder or a mystical moment that seems to stop time.

The presence and the promise of "with-ness," continuity, unreasonable joy impels us to reach out and to be. To reach out to whom? To whomever we are sent. . . . To be what? To be present and attentive. . . . To let our Christ within apprehend and be with the Christ within another, others. . . . It unfolds differently for us all. It is an event of our initiation, an initiation that goes on endlessly and is always new. It is the sacrament of ourselves, of life, of the present moment, of Emmanuel. It is the prayer within that spills into our aftermaths.

Lord, grant me this day a mission and a confidence. Free the "you" within me to see and to touch the you before me. Let me linger a while with someone, and make the long moment holy. Be with me, Lord, and open me to receive your word and your bread attentively. Then help me to be word and bread for long afterwards.

41. Friday of the Sixth Week of Easter
Acts 18:9-18 and John 16:20-23

Hemingway aficionados are familiar with his definition of courage: "Grace under pressure." Other people have said that courage is simply a matter of doing what needs to be done in spite of fear. For St. Paul, courage was a gift of the Spirit, an assurance, or reassurance, that there was really nothing to be afraid of and that God would be right there in the thick of things. "Be fearless," the Lord says. "Speak out and do not keep silence: I am with you" (Acts 18:9-10). It is the promise of Christmas, Easter, and every sacramental occasion.

All of us have received that promise, and yet we balk. We may not be brought up before Gallio the proconsul as Paul was, or pelted outside a courtroom like the respected Sosthenes. But we will be brought up in people's conversations, pummeled by their judgments and innuendoes, and beaten down by discouragement somewhere along the way. For some reason it has been ever so and will continue to be, at least until the days of a new earth and new heavens. The Lord remarked on this: that there would be grief, labor pains, sadness. But he also promised a "joy no one shall take from you" (John 16:22) and an end to torments and questions.

Courage demands the long view, a seeing through the chaos of the moment, and the confusion, to a crystal vision of love, God, the matters of eternity. There may not be many who understand or who see as we do, but we are obliged to speak our truth—if only to be true to ourselves and to the invisible One who says he is walking alongside.

Meanwhile there will also be one or two visible ones who will for a time come along—people like Priscilla and Aquila, who leave the Rome where they are unwelcome, make tents in Corinth, and travel with Paul to Syria for no other stated reason than the desire to go with him.

Paul's courage must have been buoyed by the passing vision of Christ and the long companionship of two other believers.

Lord, give me your grace when the pressure is on, along with many reminders that you are present and with me whenever I speak or do your truth. Help me, too, Lord, to seize opportunities to en_courage others by standing by them or accompanying them on a difficult journey.

∽

42. Saturday of the Sixth Week of Easter
Acts 18:23-28 and John 16:23-28

John's gospel reports that Jesus acknowledged that much of what he had said to his followers was, or seemed to be, "in veiled language" (John 16:25). There was need for more profound and clearer understanding—which, the Lord indicated, would happen in prayer, gradually. But it would come: the message "in plain words."

Apollos had had an experience of the Lord. What kind of experience it had been we don't know, but we are told that he was "an eloquent man, with a sound knowledge of the scriptures, and . . . he had been given instruction in the Way of the Lord" (Acts 18:24-25). He spoke up enthusiastically in the synagogue. When Priscilla and Aquila realized that he knew, believed, and loved but didn't know in fullness or "in plain words" about any baptism beyond John's, they took him home and catechized him. They prepared him for Spirit baptism. Apollos had his period of mystagogia, a further unfolding of the mysteries he was attempting to live and to teach. The idea was that he needed not only a life-altering experience of the Lord but also an experienced knowledge of the Holy Spirit. Thus his enthusiasm and his impulse toward evangelization could be more deeply and more authentically grounded.

After this mystagogia, Apollos could proclaim Jesus as messiah—as he had been doing right along. But he could also know with confidence that the messianic Spirit was hovering over him. He, too, would be enabled to communicate the message "in plain words."

That's really the point of it all, isn't it? That our faith must be as clear, simple, and straightforward in our own thinking as it can be; and also as unabashedly honest and detailed in our communicating it as it can be. Priscilla and Aquila both settled Apollos in and fired him up. They led him to a more lasting fire. But it took time and prayer. All three had to ask for guidance, light, and kindling—for a way to make "the new Way" brighter. Our privilege today is that not only can we sit in our parish circles for greater instruction and shared prayer but we can also tap the great resources of faith—the church's fathers and mothers, the great saints, the theologians, the spiritual guides who proclaim what they know in story and song, in scripture commentary and essay, in dissertation and confession, in popularized pamphlet and prayer. We can sit at many wise feet.

Lord, let me ask for the more and let me be a genuine seeker of wisdom, truth, and depth. Never let me settle back as if my thirst for knowing you were quenched. Keep me alive in the looking, and help me to speak what I see.

43. The Seventh Sunday of Easter

Year A—John 17:1-11
Year B—John 17:11-19
Year C—John 17:20-26

Shekinah is the heavy Hebrew glory hovering over holy things. And it is glory that the Lord speaks of this Seventh Sunday: the Father's glory, the glory belonging to the Son, the glory to be given to those who belong to God and come to oneness.

Glory is a matter of work. It is doing, praising, receiving, proclaiming, following a call. "I have glorified you on earth," the Son tells the Father, "by finishing the work that you gave me to do" (John 17:4). Glory is a matter of seeing important tasks through.

Glory is also a matter of pure being. It is living, loving, letting the wind blow, letting the world go, staying still. It is accepting the Lord's invitation to come "where I am" (John 17:24).

All of us are aware that the world has more than it needs of people who are disturbers of the peace. But we also have in our midst carriers of calm. The gracious old lady in the nursing home, the whimsical grocery store clerk, the softspoken minister, the amiable city bus driver, the child-fond pediatrician, the patient school crossing guard, the attentive politician, the persistent peacemaker, and so many, many more are persons who have a quieting aura about them. Their "secret" is often nothing more than a broader life vision than our own, a way of putting things in perspective and conserving energy for what is consequential rather than dissipating it on the altogether predictable messes and annoyances of the day. When the carrier of calm is also a person of prayer, the calm can become so powerful that we can do nothing in its face but surrender. We ourselves also become calm.

God's glory may be many things. In essence, however, it seems to be the weight of wisdom and love.

Shekinah descends into our circle and indeed enters into our being when any one of us has yielded to life's largeness, the longer view, and the wider embrace of God.

Shekinah is why Jesus could say goodbye just before betrayal, thorns, scourges, mockery, nails, and the suffocation of the cross and ask his followers and lovers to remain calm . . . to hold on . . . to come together as one. He knew that the *shekinah* of the Holy Spirit could fall upon every one of us and take us over completely, if only we open our minds, our hearts, our hands, our arms.

He prayed that breadth and wideness for us: Glory!

> *Lord, if I am not very often a carrier of calm, let the Spirit you have prayed upon me open me, in patient time, wider and wider. May I become each day a bit better at bearing your glory.*

∽

44. Monday of the Seventh Week of Easter

Acts 19:1-8 and John 16:29-33

Pam Conrad's book *Prairie Songs* tells the story of a young girl, Louisa Downing, who is among the early homesteaders in Nebraska. She lives in a leaky sod house, does rough farm work, and at a very young age witnesses miscarriage, stillbirth, violent anger, and insanity among the settlers. At one point she is speaking to a fragile city-bred new bride who finds the life unbearable. She tells her that the prairie is lonely and expansive but that she also finds something lovely and comforting in that wide loneliness. There is in Louisa not only an instinct for bare-bones survival but a vibrant and even optimistic life-force.

Among Jesus' last words to his followers we find a strange juxtaposition: "I have told you all this so that you may find peace in me. In the world you will have hardship . . ." (John 16:33). Peace and hardship are linked; they coexist, side by side. In some way they seem to depend on one another. Like Louisa's sense that there is something comforting in the insistent loneliness of the plains, the Christian's call is to discover the peace that is possible in the midst of sorrow, strife, personal pain. It is only possible, the Lord notes, because "I have conquered the world."

The life force that really matters and really sustains us is one that the early church had to discover and keep rediscovering: the Holy Spirit. Whether the gifts received were tongues, prophecies, or invincible courage, they gave endurance and staying power to those who received them. They are our gifts too: tongues to speak a word of faith and to share our perspective and our inner life; prophecies that keep our eyes on the wider panorama and our hopes on the future, prophecies of the reign of God which already is and the reign of God to come; courage to go on, knowing that we are never abandoned or alone. The Spirit tells us that there is beauty even in the wild, unsettled, heartbreaking prairie. We are invited to see and to be at peace.

Lord, lend me the long view. Let me see beyond today's pain into the future possibility. At the same time, help me to see whatever beauty there is in the present moment, in whatever is before me. Give me the courage and comfort of your peaceful Spirit.

∽

45. Tuesday of the Seventh Week of Easter
Acts 20:17-27 and John 17:1-11

Presidents of the United States have at times given memorable farewell addresses, and they have always, it seems, taken pains with their inaugurals. Today's readings replay for us farewells by Paul and by the Lord. Paul is setting out for Jerusalem, knowing "that imprisonment and persecution await me" (Acts 20:23). Jesus is on the edge of his "hour" and expresses gratitude to the Father that he has come to the point of "finishing the work that you gave me to do" (John 17:4). Both farewells are poignant, and both Paul and Jesus acknowledge by implication the pain that will be felt by their disciples.

But they speak more than a moving farewell. They also deliver an inaugural. In his Holy Thursday discourse, the Lord passes the torch, recounting in his prayer that he has left three things to his followers: a message (the good news of the reign of God); a bonding and belonging (community in Christ, in God); and eternal life. Paul similarly takes his leave with the reminder that he has unfolded for the Ephesians "the whole of God's purpose" (Acts 20:27). It is left to them to live out this purpose and design and to discern its further implications.

John F. Kennedy's inaugural address in January of 1961 hailed the passing of the torch "to a new generation." Our tradition in Christ and in Paul—and in the long history of the church which has followed—indicates that we, too, have been handed the torchlight of faith and that we are called to pass it on. In our own way, we are called to communicate the message of the reign of God, to invite others to bond and belong with us in that reign, and to point the way to eternal life. Those three ancient Greek words which are said to characterize what it is to be church fit here: *kerygma* (the preaching), *koinonia* (community), and *diakonia* (service). As we witness, bond, and serve, we bring on the reign of God, create church, and give one another a taste of what eternal life might be.

Lord, let me say hello and goodbye, goodbye and hello, by being conscious and attentive to your underlying purposes, mindful of that reign of God which you proclaim. Make me responsive to the opportunities I have to bear your message, to help others sense their belonging, and to serve the causes of both time and eternity.

∽

46. Wednesday of the Seventh Week of Easter

Acts 20:28-38 and John 17:11-19

"HUGS NOT DRUGS" broadcasts one of those bumper stickers which promote preventive nurturance on the part of parents. The idea behind the slogan is very much the idea of the reading from Acts and the section from John's gospel for today: the idea that we are called to *manifest* our caring and to be vigilant in the face of the forces of uncaring and destruction—the forces of evil.

The Lord demonstrated his love for the disciples at the last supper—with his eucharist, the feet washing, and these last words of love, friendship, and prayer which are recorded in John 14-17. Paul demonstrated his love for the Ephesians by his example, his dedication, and his farewell advice to them. They, in turn, wept at his departure, covering him with hugs and kisses.

Both the Lord and Paul were advocates of a *vigilant* style of caring. Neither wanted their followers and friends to live in a huggy, kissy, fluffily naive world. They wanted them to be aware that simple, honest, tender prayer and care were not only nice in themselves but necessary in the face of the world's "fierce wolves" (Acts 20:29). The world could be something the flock needed at times to be protected from, the Lord reminded them. There were unsavory sorts, Paul recalled, who were experts at "coming forward with a travesty of the truth on their lips to induce the disciples to follow them" (Acts 20:30). There was also the lure of silver and gold and gorgeous clothes.

It takes no astonishing insight for us to realize that the same situation prevails today. There is simple, innocent love and magnanimous goodness. There are gentle, sincere, kindly people anywhere. But there are also tremendous forces of moral erosion in our midst. None of us is at a loss to name some of the ferocious wolves howling at our door and threatening the well-being of us and our children. We need to "be on guard" ourselves, and we need to watch out for one another.

That is why we have sponsors at our baptisms and confirmations. That is why we have mentors, confessors, counselors, and spiritual friends. We are called to pray for and to cherish one another as spiritual treasure. And we are invited—by the example of a Lord who knelt to wash our grubby feet and a Paul who received a lavish manifestation of affection—to love demonstratively.

When, Lord, have I failed to express love when I should have let my feelings be known? When, Lord, have I left others at risk or to their own devices when I could have *offered an arm for support, a presence for encouragement? Help me, Lord, to be a vigilant nurturer of my friends and your <u>followers</u>, old and young.*

∽

47. Thursday of the Seventh Week of Easter
Acts 22:30; 23:6-11 and John 17:20-26

We can almost picture Paul standing there before the Sanhedrin with his tongue in his cheek as he plays into their favorite Pharisee-Sadducee squabbles about the possibility of resurrection and the existence of the spirit world. Was he setting them up and stalling for time? Quite possibly. The upshot of it is that he ends the day realizing that he will indeed have to go to Rome—not so much to defend himself as to testify to the Lord's aliveness as he had in Jerusalem.

It was a very-much-alive Lord who both caused Paul's troubles and gave him courage. It was the same Lord who had spoken of glory and living on as he passed the vigil of his crucifixion.

As Paul played out his path from one persecutor, one commander, one jailkeeper to another, we can imagine that he saw it with a larger vision. Even while his life was in jeopardy, Paul could see the silliness of the persecution games. In a way, his beginning his "defense" by blurting out that he is a Pharisee and that he believes in the resurrection is a bemused way of instigating more of the game. As he watched, Paul could also see the widening circles. The word wouldn't be silenced by a fussing Sanhedrin. The word wouldn't be locked up in a jail. Paul, among others, would carry the word to Rome. And the resurrection would prove real, even as jails filled and blood spilled in arenas.

The Lord had prayed that the Father's love would live

on in his friends. He asked that he himself would live on. The tongue-in-cheek Paul, watching Sadducees sputtering against raisings and angels, also could be dead serious about an awesome truth. He had written about it elsewhere: "It is no longer I, but Christ living in me" (Galatians 2:20). Paul was certain that Christ was living—not as angel, not as spirit, but as the risen One . . . in Paul, in his brothers and sisters in the Lord, in his successors, whom we are today.

Lord, even when I can laugh at the shenanigans of those who don't believe and the short-sightedness of those who do, keep me focused on the everlasting vision—the ever-widening circles that radiate out from you.

∽

48. *Friday of the Seventh Week of Easter*
Acts 25:13-21 and John 21:15-19

Both Peter and Paul had ample forewarning that fidelity to Jesus and perseverance in mission would be something for which they would pay. Peter had it from the Lord directly, in the last encounter recorded by John. After he had answered affirmatively three times to the Lord's question—"Do you love me?"—Peter was told that his mission to feed and tend the flock would cause him to be carried off and stretched. Ultimately, tradition tells us, he was stretched out on a cross. Paul had to face a procession of accusers and judges because of his insistence that Jesus had been dead but was alive. He went from chief priests and elders, to Pharisees and Sadducees, to Felix, to Festus, to King Agrippa and Bernice and spent much time under arrest before, finally, he also was executed.

Msgr. John Esseff, who spent considerable time in Lebanon working with Catholic Relief Services, has told of hearing the bishop at his childhood confirmation remark to the boys and girls that they were not likely to face physical martyrdom for their faith; instead, they could expect to be challenged and misunderstood. After Msgr. Esseff had the grim task of identifying the body of a Dutch priest, his friend, who had been tortured and then thrown into a well to die a slow death, he said that no American or Western European should ever be led to believe that he or she might not have to pay for faith with his or her life. Esseff himself was finally recalled from the Mideast when church officials decided that his presence there had become futile and a constant source of threat. There had already been too many deaths.

Most of us don't imagine that faith will cost us our lives or our freedom. But Msgr. Esseff reminds everyone to whom he preaches that it *can*.

The question is not just whether we are capable of heroism. It is whether we can hold fast to the faith when the criticisms, challenges, incomprehensions, and perhaps ridicule begin and then mount. Do we stay with our Christian convictions or begin to hedge, to compromise, to water down? . . .

Lord, as I gaze at the image of your cross, let me remember that you die again in our midst today. I am one, Lord, with your martyrs—in the Mideast, in Central America, in South Africa, in Liberia, or wherever they may be. Lord, I fear even the thought of death squads, torture, brainwashing, or even passing emotional pain. But let my fear, Lord, recall that there is only one final fear: the loss of you. Help me to hold on, even till death.

49. Saturday of the Seventh Week of Easter
Acts 28:16-20, 30-31 and John 21:20-25

There are a number of places in scripture where affection spills over in abundance. The last verse of John's gospel is a mixture of a disciple's affection, which has become almost speechless, and an awe which cannot find words big enough: "There was much else that Jesus did; if it were written down in detail, I do not suppose the world itself would hold all the books that would be written" (John 21:25).

Peter and John and, later, Paul found that there was never an end to what could be said about the Lord. There were not only soulful memories, but there were new and surprising experiences of his action and presence. Even under house arrest, even in chains, Paul could not stop speaking and writing about the one he called "the hope of Israel" (Acts 28:20).

Jesus inspires our affection and awe still. That is why we have images of him, artist's renderings in pictures and crucifixes and statues, in our homes and churches and museums. That is why we purchase greeting cards that tell the "Footprints" story or retell the impact of "One Solitary Life." That is why we find ourselves and hear others speaking of him in the present tense.

Every one of us is, if we realize it, "the disciple whom Jesus loved" (John 21:20) and loves still. Every one of us can acquire a reputation as Paul did for "welcoming all who came to visit him" (Acts 28:30) and sharing the Lord with them.

Faith, in the end, is never just a matter of intellectual understanding and agreement with a body of religious teaching. It is also a matter of affection, of letting the heart be touched and being free enough to tell, at times, where the awe and the tenderness has come from.

Lord, let the many things for which I am grateful fill me with affection for you, and give me words to tell the story to anyone who has an open heart and a willingness to listen. And let me keep discovering the awe of who you are and all you do.

50. Pentecost Sunday

Acts 2:1-11
1 Corinthians 12:3-7, 12-13
John 20:19-23

In one of the more memorable commencement addresses ever given at Berwick Area Senior High School in Pennsylvania, an executive of U.S. Steel, a graduate of the same school, introduced the students to the Hindu "Trimurite," the three great gods who are not one and not a Trinity—Brahma, Shiva, and Vishnu: the Creator, the Destroyer, and the Preserver. These three life forces, the speaker suggested, represent choices we make about how to use our energies and how to live on the planet.

Pentecost presents a Trinity to us which is all Creator and Preserver. There is no Destroyer but instead a Redeemer, who can be said also to be a "Transformer." The Holy Spirit comes to us as both Preserver and Transformer too: Preserver of our life with God, Preserver of the church to which she has given birth, Transformer of our scattered and diverse selves into "one body," and Transformer too of our sinfulness into forgiveness.

The second reading tells us that our baptism has brought us into oneness, a oneness of faith which prompts us to declare this one sentence in many different tongues, in diverse personal styles: "Jesus is Lord" (1 Corinthians 12:3). Our communion, our invitation to receive "the same Spirit to drink" (1 Corinthians 12:13) and to be the "one body," strengthens, forgives, renews, and sends us forth to use our whole selves, with our many gifts, "for the general good" (1 Corinthians 12:7). The Spirit once again enlivens us at our own Pentecost, the day or night of our confirmation, with a force that impels us outward. We are "filled" first, then moved to "express" ourselves, and in so doing proclaim—almost brashly—"the marvels of God" (Acts 2: 4, 11). The meaning and reality of our "Spiritedness" take shape over a lifetime. Meanwhile the Spirit comes, too, to renew and redirect us in the sacrament of forgiveness, through human agency, with a power given by the Lord, the power of peace.

The thing that is astonishing is that these sacramental outpourings of the Spirit, the force of the Spirit's manifestations and the power of the Spirit's promptings, come to us and yet still leave us free. The Spirit comes with a gentle power and prompting. We can almost fail to notice the Spirit's preserving and transforming, even as it is happening.

However the Spirit comes to us, however the Spirit keeps coming, she calls us to Godliness. And that Godliness calls us to join in the energies of creating and preserving and transforming, of renewing the face of the earth, and of bonding one to another in the name of the Lord who breathes life and love.

> *Continue, o Comforter, Light, Remaker, and Guide, to show me how I am called each day to live lovingly, to give creatively, to make a difference in my world, and to be—with so varied and many—your church. Keep us growing and gifting, on and on.*
>
> *Amen. Alleluia. Amen.*

And mystagogia, with all of life after Easter, goes on.